IT IS GOOD FOR US TO BE HERE

IT IS GOOD FOR US TO BE HERE

Catholic Religious Institutes as
NGOs at the United Nations

Editors: Emeka Xris Obiezu, OSA;

Joan F. Burke, SNDdeN; and

Cecile Meijer, RSCJ

To order additional copies of this book, contact:
Xlibris
1-888-795-4274
www.Xlibris.com
Orders@Xlibris.com
722029

CONTENTS

SWORDS INTO PLOUGHSHARES; SPEARS INTO
PRUNING HOOKS
    The Pivotal Role of NGOs on the World Stage
    Foreword by Professor Joy U. Ogwu
    (Nigeria Ambassador to the United Nations)   1

INTRODUCTION
    Emeka Xris Obiezu, OSA   3

THE INDWELLING PRESENCE IN OUR
WORLD TODAY
    Cecile Meijer, RSCJ   6

REMEMBERING THE BEGINNINGS
    A History of RUN
    Marie Elena Dio, SC   10

BEYOND PLUMBING! LONG-TERM ENGAGEMENT!
    Reality and Challenges of Religious Institutes'
    New Identity as NGOs
    Joan F. Burke, SNDdeN (D.Phil., Oxon.)   14

THE SIGNIFICANCE OF PLACE – UNITED NATIONS
    Partnering Religious Congregations with UNICEF
    Deirdre Mullan, RSM, PhD   22

MULTILEVEL COMMUNITY WITNESSING
    Augustinians International
    John Paul Szura, OSA   26

WE ARE ONE HUMAN FAMILY, ONE EARTH
COMMUNITY
    Sisters of Charity Federation
        Caroljean Willie, SC, PhD   32

PASSION FOR JESUS, PASSION FOR LIFE
    Enter the Passionists in the Heart of Politics
        Kevin Dance, CP   38

UNANIMA:
    Bringing the "Feminine Soul" to the UN
        Michele Morek, OSU   46

HEALING PRESENCE OF JESUS IN THE
WOUNDED WORLD
    Medical Mission Sisters
        Celine Paramundayil MMS   51

ESTABLISHING JUSTICE THAT IS EFFECTIVE
IN TODAY'S WORLD
    Maryknoll Sisters at the United Nations
        Elizabeth Zwareva, MM   55

WORKING FOR JUSTICE, ACTING FOR PEACE
    Loretto Community's Global Advocacy at the UN
        Sally Dunne, Comember   59

STILL DOING WHAT NEEDS TO BE DONE
    International Presentation Association
        Mary Margaret Mooney, PBVM   63

EPILOGUE:
    A Catholic NGO Reflection on Life, Leadership, and
    Community at United Nations
        Joseph Cornelius Donnelly
        Permanent Delegate to the United Nations
        CARITAS Internationalis   67

We are grateful to Congregation of the Mission, Sisters of Charity of Cincinnati and Passionists International for funding this publication.

SWORDS INTO PLOUGHSHARES; SPEARS INTO PRUNING HOOKS

The Pivotal Role of NGOs on the World Stage

Foreword by Professor Joy U. Ogwu (Nigeria Ambassador to the United Nations)

The point of departure of the UN Charter aspires to save "succeeding generations from the scourge of war, which . . . has brought untold sorrow to mankind." As the world drama unfolds over the years, it has become evident that state actors alone cannot successfully address global problems. Indeed, in contemporary times, nongovernmental actors have become not only relevant but also legitimate actors in the larger policy process.

Within the context of the international community, NGOs have become an essential part of the life of the UN. Their preoccupation touches virtually every aspect of global politics—from pandemics and poverty to peace and security. They give the UN organization confidence that its programs reach their desired targets, especially those of the world's poor and disadvantaged. Indeed, the NGOs attempt to keep the UN informed with realities in theaters of operation.

Groups from Catholic traditions, especially those of institutes of religious life, have been the most influential faith-based NGOs. Together with other religious, spiritual, or faith-based NGOs, they have not only played a range of positive roles but have also affected UN decision making and its approach to global issues by the moral and ethical consciousness they bring to the entire process of peace, security, and development.

In their long history of activities in education and care of the poor, members of institutes of religious life have contributed immensely to the development of the world's human resource, including mine. More significantly, they have been a force for peace and justice. They were the pioneers in technologies, literacy, and medical knowledge in many parts of the world. In our times, they continue to explore the frontiers of knowledge and understanding.

Nowhere is their constructive role in promoting the common good more evident than at the United Nations, the heart of international politics. This study, *It Is Good for Us to Be Here*, epitomizes the unique advocacy work of an organized transnational actor. Even more significantly, the selfless, spiritual, and prayerful support they provide as a duty to those who serve in the international community will remain an invaluable source of strength.

I am honored to write the foreword to this inspiring and encouraging reflection, conveyed in a truly simple and lucid prose. I believe it will help promote a better understanding of the nexus between faith life and working for social development. Perhaps it is through such a range of positive roles that we can truly beat our "swords into ploughshares."

INTRODUCTION

Emeka Xris Obiezu, OSA

Among the groups of Roman Catholic nongovernmental organizations (NGOs) at the United Nations are religious institutes of men and women who have come to see the intergovernmental process as a key arena of advocacy on behalf of those they serve. Religious institutes have an enduring tradition of concern for those living in poverty, demonstrated by their commitment to the direct service of the immediate needs of the people living on the margins and the underside of society. Given the enormity and complexity of the sufferings of growing numbers in contemporary society, men and women religious saw how important it is to identify and address the systemic causes of the deepening poverty and ever-increasing inequality which seemingly have become embedded in social structures. Responding boldly to these "signs of the times" requires a profound paradigm shift as integral to the call of Vatican II to a radical renewal of religious life based on the spirit of congregations' founders and foundresses.[1]

Women and men religious share profoundly the hopes and anxieties of the peoples of today's world. Their experience and

---

[1]   "Decree on the Up-to-Date Renewal of Religious Life: Perfectae Caritatis, #2," ed. Austin Flannery, vol. 1 of *Vatican Council II: The Conciliar and Post Conciliar Documents New Revised Edition* (Northport, New York: Costello Publishing Company, 2004), 612.

commitment impel them to make their own these concerns. They cannot stand by as mere spectators. They are called to be the bearers of God's dream for his people, especially for the downtrodden and indeed the entire creation. In addition to their continued providing for immediate needs of the impoverished and marginalized, they have searched to see how they might become more effective agents of change by promoting justice in societies where they live and work. This has led many religious to become more involved in the processes of formulation of social policies to bring about structural changes as a matter of justice. They recognized that working with other civil society groups at the United Nations offered an opportunity to be effective advocates for more just global structures out of the universal solidarity with those whom they serve and to support the work of their members on the ground in the field.

This apostolate could be taken for granted by some Catholics. However, a good many others, including some of their own communities, are still somewhat unfamiliar with the length and breadth of this project. They question the religious significance of such witnessing with respect to their call to follow Christ in chastity, poverty, and obedience. Not all readily see the urgent need to integrate more appropriately into pastoral ministry international issues and a global dimension. This is what has informed this project.

The reflections in this booklet articulate the nature and significance of a UN apostolate in a simple and clear manner. It is written for members of various groups of religious men and women and others outside this circle who may wish to understand better both the scope and possible impact of advocacy work at the UN. The historical descriptions and theological analyses provided here guide the ordinary Catholic reader, those in the pew, to appreciate and assess the relevance of a UN apostolate in the realization of the salvific mission of the Catholic Church today. That includes enabling them to appreciate the social question as a worldwide issue as well as an everyday faith life issue. The importance given to grounding global advocacy in the local activities of the memberships of these religious institutes demonstrates how integrally related the principles of universal solidarity and subsidiarity are—the genuine concern for the global and for the local, respectively.

Contributors are either current or past representatives of their various groups at the United Nations, with rich experiences and deep knowledge of their various charisms and spirituality. For the most part they are representatives of international institutes who are involved in a wide range of ministries. These authors bring with them the various identities and theological self-understandings, spiritualities, and charisms of their different groups. The easy to read narrative describes who they are, what brought them to the UN, their activities, and their hopes. They offer their reflections on their achievements, lessons learned, challenges, prospects, and how this mission is a religious apostolate and not just some mere social activism.

This booklet would serve as handy document for animators of justice and peace and UN representatives of religious institutes during education programs for their members. There is a hope that it might be used in parishes and Catholic schools for education on Christian social responsibility. It may also stimulate greater collaboration and engagement with lay organizations who are accredited as NGOs at the United Nations.

THE INDWELLING PRESENCE IN OUR WORLD TODAY*

Cecile Meijer, RSCJ

As a Religious of the Sacred Heart who has represented the Society of the Sacred Heart at the United Nations (UN) for more than twelve years, I sometimes wonder where God is in the face of so much suffering and pain around the world. Thanks to instant communication, images of boat refugees adrift on the high seas and reports of hunger and malnourished children due to failed crops and drought are just one click away on our remote at home, in the car, at work, or at school. Our world is also becoming increasingly violent. Armed violence manifests itself in our cities, violent extremism floods our living rooms when we watch primetime news, and violently contagious diseases threaten the existence of whole communities and countries as the recent Ebola crisis has shown.

At the same time, our world is highly interconnected, offering both opportunities and challenges. International trade, financial markets, the internet and global mobility, in general, have all contributed to previously unimaginable progress and wealth. But the advances have been unequal, indiscriminately so when looked at from a global perspective. More than one billion people still live in extreme poverty today—that is about 18 percent of the world

---

* This chapter is based on the Digby Stuart Annual Lecture delivered by the author at the University of Roehampton, London, UK, on March 19, 2015.

population who cannot care for their most basic human needs. Approximately 748 million people have no access to clean drinking water, while a good one-third of the world still has no access to decent sanitation. How can we allow these scandals to continue?

Our world is out of balance—so where is our solidarity, our focus on the common good? How do we as Christians live out our preferential option for the poor, recognizing on a daily basis the human dignity of each person? We seem to have lost that sense of *ubuntu*, of which Archbishop Desmond Tutu from South Africa often speaks. *Ubuntu* is best described with the African proverb "I am because we are, and we are because I am." In other words, we are not islands but part of a single common humanity; we depend on each other. A lived sense of solidarity is the expression of such oneness. But what is the spiritual root of such solidarity? What is the basis of this notion of right relationships—justice in the social, economic, and environmental dimensions of all life?

Scripture is explicit in calling each of us "to love God with all your heart, with all your mind and with all of your strength, and to love your neighbor as yourself" (Matthew 22:37; Mark 12:30; Luke 10:27). This commandment to love God above all things and our neighbor as ourselves speaks to me not only of the transcendent God, God beyond our imagining, but also of the immanent God, the God within each of us. The presence of God within all of creation is not only repeated over and over again in Scripture, this life-giving breath of God has been the sustaining energy throughout our human history. Thomas Merton articulates this reality of the "God within" in these words: "God has, so to speak, put something of the divine goodness in everything. There are holy sparks in all created beings. The human task is to see these things and to liberate the divine sparks in creation by praise, love and joy."[2]

For me this acknowledgment that God is the heartbeat in all of creation is the ultimate way to peace. Heartbeat is of course a strong image in the Sacred Heart educational tradition. Respect for each living being and organism on planet Earth—persons, animals, plants, etc.—as God's home breaks down walls and prejudices.

---

[2] Thomas Merton, *The Springs of Contemplation, A Retreat at the Abbey of Gethsemani* (Notre Dame, Indiana: Ave Maria Press, 1992), 151.

What it boils down to is the realization that if God lives in me, then God lives equally in my neighbor and in everything that breathes—everything that is. This awareness has huge implications. For example, as Christians we are continuously invited to make more room for God, to widen the flaps of our tent, so to speak. But if God lives equally in other people, doesn't this also mean that we are called to make it possible for other persons to widen the flaps of their tent by living in more dignity? Doesn't that challenge us to work for structural change so that the growing inequalities within and among countries can be addressed?

It is exactly at this intersection of love of God and love of neighbor that working for justice comes in. If justice is understood in the biblical sense of right relationships, love lived out comes forth as justice, mercy, and humility. For example, if we really recognize Christ in the migrant on a rickety boat trying to reach a safe haven in Italy, Greece or Malaysia, we cannot turn away because we are donor- or suffering-fatigued—we cannot resort once more to the globalization of indifference, as Pope Francis has called it, because in each migrant Christ has a home. And how about people living in poverty in slums, barrios, and favelas? Are our eyes and hearts open to acknowledge God within each of these persons as we ponder how to feed, house, educate, employ, and transport half of the world's population living in overburdened cities today, knowing that urbanization will only grow further in the near future? Do we hear God sighing and crying out for more dignity when we read that 13 percent of the global labor force of young people aged 15–24 is unemployed, not counting those who have given up looking for decent work or are working in their country's informal economy?

Recognizing that God lives in the woman and girl being trafficked; that Love dwells in the immigrant desperate for water under the scorching desert sun; that Christ sleeps in the park because there is still no room in the inn—recognizing the divine presence as indwelling in each of these realities not only changes us but can also change the world. What all these examples have in common is that they are about ruptures in relationships, a breaking down of our oneness as humanity. And we have the individual and collective power to do something about that.

In 1971, the World Synod of Catholic Bishops in the document called *Justice in the World* stated, "Action on behalf of justice and participation in the transformation of the world fully appears to us as a constitutive dimension of the preaching of the Gospel, or, in other words, of the Church's mission for the redemption of the human race and its liberation from every oppressive situation."[3]

Isn't that what acknowledging Christ in our neighbor means in essence? Liberating the other from every oppressive situation? This is what motivates many faith-based nongovernmental organizations (NGOs) at the UN such as the Society of the Sacred Heart to keep on pressing for people-centered and creation-centered development. The Society of the Sacred Heart has been at the UN as an NGO since 2003. Because the UN is an intergovernmental organization, its members are individual nation states. NGOs are not UN members nor are NGO representatives a part of the UN's staff. As a part of "We the Peoples of the United Nations," NGOs are present to knock on diplomats' doors and make a lot of noise, urging them to listen to the people's voices.

As a human organization, the UN is far from perfect. Sometimes we, NGO representatives, find an open door; other times the issues are too complex for quick answers, requiring instead a slow process of collaboration and perseverance. In *The Economist*'s "The World in 2015," Edward Carr wrote, "The world is messy. As they say, success in politics is not perfection; it is going from failure to failure without loss of enthusiasm."[4] Isn't that what hope is all about—unleashing ever more deeply the Indwelling Presence in all of creation so as to let hope speak and transform our world from within?

---

3   Synod of Bishops, *Justice in the World*, 1971, paragraph 6.

4   Edward Carr, "World disorder," in *The Economist: The World in 2015*, 20.

REMEMBERING THE BEGINNINGS

A History of RUN

Marie Elena Dio, SC

Prior to 1997 there were just a handful of Catholic religious congregations represented as nongovernmental organizations (NGOs) at the United Nations (UN). Among them were Franciscans International, Congregations of St. Joseph, School Sisters of Notre Dame, Presentation Sisters, Loretto Sisters, Medical Missionaries, Sisters of the Good Shepherd, and perhaps one or two others. That's all. Each representative learned how, pretty much on her/his own, to navigate the complexity that is the United Nations: several hundred cultures, the maze of corridors, numerous departments—each covering many issues, long lists of acronyms, unending meetings, reams of publications, etc.

Attendance at monthly UN Department of Public Information (DPI) sessions and common lunch breaks gave some representatives the occasional opportunity to find and meet one another. In 1998, three NGO representatives (a Sister of St. Joseph, a Dominican, a Sister of Charity) began to schedule monthly meetings for the purpose of mutual support. They began to gather other representatives and invited each new congregational NGO representative to "come be with us."

The International Catholic Organization (ICO) office initially served as the gathering place until early 2000s when the group outgrew the available space. As the number of religious congregations at the UN increased—seven, fifteen, twenty-five, and eventually more than forty—the desire for a more organized agenda as a means for sharing methodology and techniques and for offering orientation for new NGOs arose. At the same time, it was important to all to preserve the supportive aspect of our meetings.

As the size of the group increased, meetings became a bit less informal. Careful to maintain a distinction from the Committee of Religious NGOs—an umbrella of all faith-based NGOs present at the UN—a group name was chosen: Religious at the UN (RUN). Prepared agendas, chosen chairs, secretaries, etc. and serious conversations about the purpose, future work, meeting format, and group membership emerged.

In the initial years, the main purposes for the monthly meeting were for mutual support and to provide a beginning place for new NGO representatives of congregations. Conversations often centered on how to connect religious charisms with UN work. From the beginning, after serious discussions, it was agreed that the group was *not* a Catholic bloc or caucus, not a substitute for working with nonreligious NGOs and committees, and not a place for creating agreements or interventions on UN issues. This was to be a place for support, prayer, relaxation, and sharing of information and expertise. It was to be different from NGO committees in that we would not be focusing on specific UN issues beyond sharing information on upcoming meetings, conferences, and general points of interest.

Several conversations on the subject of membership in RUN were held over the ensuing years. A few other Catholic NGOs expressed interest in being part of the group. Since many of the RUN members also held membership in and attended meetings of the ICO, it was agreed that RUN gatherings would be restricted to members of religious congregations. These, it was felt, have specific needs regarding charisms, relationship with the Vatican State (Holy See Permanent Observer Mission), and theological interpretations. Congregations' representatives would continue to give support to other Catholic NGOs through our attendance at ICO. RUN membership and attendance might include lay associates serving as a congregation's main NGO representative but not nonreligious interns or visitors.

The issue of working with the Holy See office at the UN arose several times, particularly during the Commission on the Status of Women (CSW) meetings. The Holy See is not an NGO but a recognized governmental body. NGOs are somewhat restricted in their affiliation with governments. It was therefore decided that as NGOs we would work with the Holy See Mission in the same way as we would work with any other governmental body.

Having decided what we were not, many characteristics and needs arose to capture our united attention and interest: How do we motivate, educate, and include general congregational membership in the UN ministry? What means of communication do we use with them? How do we set up and maintain a website? How do we format, use, or transmit newsletters? What methods do we use in orienting visitors, interns or new representatives? What are effective and acceptable lobbying techniques? What are the inter-linkages among congregations' foci? How do we connect our members in the field? How do various issues intersect one another? The meeting also provided opportunities for signing on to one another's written interventions and for scheduling one-on-one sharing sessions.

Annually RUN spends a day together off campus in retreat where we ponder the importance of "being" before "doing"; the preeminence of UN work over our own reputations or resume-building; and the necessity of ensuring that our ministry flowed out of a strong prayer life. Special holiday lunches and a late spring vacation day also provide us with time to simply enjoy one another's company.

The existence of RUN has provided congregational NGOs a body for contact with the International Union of Superiors General (UISG, USG), Commission for Justice, Peace, and Integrity of Creation (JPIC), Rome as well as with our NGO representatives stationed in Geneva. Practical needs, such as individual housing opportunities, funding opportunities, office sharing, and sharing of UN visitor passes, are also facilitated.

In 2009 it was decided to prepare a manual of useful information for future NGO representatives. It contains

Qualifications of the Main NGO Representative
Major and Continuing Responsibilities of the NGO
    Representative
Skills and Abilities

In the most recently conducted review adopted at the January 2015 meeting, RUN retains its original and primary goals of serving as opportunity to reflect upon the common NGO mission of all the member congregations. Each monthly meeting is organically structured and contains a substantive segment and always allows for connecting with one another in flexibility and spontaneity.

BEYOND PLUMBING! LONG-TERM ENGAGEMENT!

Reality and Challenges of Religious Institutes' New Identity as NGOs

Joan F. Burke, SNDdeN (D.Phil., Oxon.)

When I was invited to become the first representative of our congregation as an accredited NGO at the United Nations in 2002, I was living in rural Nigeria. I had been working in different countries of Africa for almost twenty years and was looking forward to a sabbatical back in the States. Among the things I wanted to do were crash courses in auto mechanics, plumbing and electricity—all very relevant to my life situation at the time. And so, for me at that point, relocating to New York and working at the UN seemed to have no relationship with my life at all. Of course, for most of us who belong to religious congregations, when asked to take up a work by the Congregational Leadership Team we do not feel very free to refuse. And so it was that I said good-bye to the prospect of a sabbatical and relocated to New York. There I found myself in a very different world. Initially, I felt overwhelmed. So to cope I put on my "hat" as a trained social anthropologist and tried to learn the system and what our place was as a religious congregation accredited to the Economic and Social Council (ECOSOC) at the UN. Slowly, I began to realize that being an NGO opened me up to an unbeknownst identity and an unfolding sense of mission on a very different level of our justice call.

All of us have multiple identities. We can at one and the same time be children, parents and grandparents, spouses and in-laws, breadwinners and housekeepers, athletes and musicians, students and teachers, government workers, and members of civil society. All these identities affect both how we understand ourselves and how others see us. Taking on a new identity can very much impact our awareness of ourselves and reveal to us and others added dimensions of who we are. We realize that we have assumed new responsibilities into which we must grow.

For eight years (2002–2010) I served as the NGO representative of the Sisters of Notre Dame de Namur (SNDdeN) at the United Nations in New York. I want to offer here my reflections on how our becoming a recognized nongovernmental organization (NGO) with the United Nations in 2002 made me begin to rethink the work and services we as a congregation have been carrying out across the globe for over two hundred years. I would imagine this is not unique to us as SNDs and may well suggest our yet nascent experiences are similar to other religious congregations. For me, it has made concrete a significant "sign of our times" of the post–Vatican II era; even as we now belong to what has become a "world church," we have a responsibility to be global women.

Very early I did see that we are not nongovernmental organizations in the more usual way. By the very fact of our being Catholic sisters, we have made a lifelong commitment to the organization. As a consequence of this free choice, our being a part of the group very much defines our understanding of ourselves. In contrast to some of my NGO colleagues at the UN, I did not see myself as an employee of an NGO, but in a real sense I was—as are other members of the Sisters of Notre Dame de Namur—an embodiment of the organization which I represented. I was caught short when another NGO representative expressed her amazement that I did not have to run by a board in a far off place the oral and written statements I drafted for UN meetings. I heard myself reply, "But I am a full member of the Sisters of Notre Dame. This is my life."

As Sisters of Notre Dame, the majority of us are trained teachers involved in a wide variety of services to people on all five continents: formal and informal education, community-based and institutional health services, rural development, youth work, empowerment of persons living in poverty and of women, and increasingly, advocacy. Through all of these we aim to be for others' sisters and as sister an enabling presence. Gradually, though, we have come to see that as necessary as this work is, it is but a drop in the bucket and a temporary "Band-Aid." The needs will remain far greater than we can ever address, and more and more of our sisters and brothers will become impoverished if we do not find ways to change the larger global structures that create ever deeper chasms between the "haves" and "have-nots" of today's world.

Before I became an NGO representative, I spent close to twenty years in different countries of Africa (the Democratic Republic of the Congo, Nigeria, and Kenya). At that time the very idea of being part of an NGO was not at all a part of my consciousness. Oftentimes we purposefully kept our distance from NGOs that frequently seemed to be just a "front" for ambitious politicians who wanted to build up a constituency. Local, hands-on, grassroots, service-providing NGOs were few. Today, after working in an environment where my own organization is recognized as an NGO, I have quite a different perspective on what being a nongovernmental organization means. I now see that an NGO can simply be a recognized group of ordinary members of civil society who join together to improve their societies and influence government policies, so they are more people centered. Before, I had not ever thought of my belonging to civil society as particularly significant in my capacity to be an agent of change.

I also certainly was not too keen in the different societies where I lived to entertain and make any great efforts to dialogue with politicians, who rarely impressed me as really having any commitment to those of their people who lived in deep poverty. However, with my colleagues in the NGO community in New York, I came to appreciate that the only influence we could have in the intergovernmental process was through persuasion and capitalizing on our moral authority. Governments knew we were representing the folk on the ground who were doing the spade work among their people through education, health services, and development programs. Many a time, I was touched by government representatives in informal settings thanking us for speaking out on issues they did not have the "permission" of their governments to address. When we had an opportunity to meet one another as people outside the formal corridors of the UN, I often found we shared many deep, common values, even across very different faith traditions. We NGOs came to understand the pressures on governments and their many limitations, but we also recognized their discreet efforts to open doors for us so that we could speak our truth. UN staffers did this for us as well. They saw us as spokespersons on behalf of the ordinary people on the ground, especially those living in poverty and without any voice. Somehow they instinctively knew we were sincere in our commitment to live out of a universal sisterhood.

Those years of serving as the first representative of our group as an NGO at the UN has also given me insights into a dimension of our identity beyond the fact that we are a values-based and faith-inspired group of long-time direct service providers and advocates for social development. We are a group of committed women who have learned to support one another for the long haul. I still find myself saying that those working to change social structures "have to be radical believers in incremental change." Even as this can be said of large bureaucracies such as the United Nations, women religious have a long experience to know that it is equally true of the Catholic Church!

Sharing these thoughts may stimulate others to reflect on how we can all better foster the development of civil society across the globe in the service of people-centered policies and programs. NGOs such as ours are often very much appreciated for this both in the field and in the intergovernmental arena.

In my view, religious congregations such as ours seem to be particularly effective in the NGO community at the UN through the many committees and working groups for several reasons:

1. Many of us come from professions (education, community organizing) which have given us skills in helping others to become engaged.

2. Our members come from many cultures across the world so we have had to work at learning to dialogue across differences to seek common understandings.
3. We carry a strong conviction that everyone brings to the table different gifts and skills that can be complementary and contribute to the work of the whole.
4. Our "organizational culture" has helped us see the need for group work and collaboration.
5. By and large, we have had to learn to do what we do on "shoestring" budgets.
6. By a free choice, we have made a life commitment to serve others out of our common sisterhood.

In addition to these, from the times of our founders and foundresses, the long-term commitment of our sisters in education and health fields—often in very marginalized areas—have convinced us of the possibility of social change. We tend to take some of these "corporate gifts" for granted. Maybe we need to think more deliberately how they can be used to greater effect in broader circles beyond ourselves for the service of today's social agenda.

As with many similar NGOs, as sisters our main concern is to promote the common good of all the people we work with across the world and not that of our organizations themselves. What impels us is the gospel agenda. Our sights are not limited by national boundaries or what governments often describe as their national interest. The issues that concern us stop at no one's borders: hunger, poverty, discrimination and social exclusion, lack of education and basic health, violence, and the abuse of human rights. For this reason we seek to join forces with all groups who are similarly focused to address these concerns and assist governments to develop policies and action plans which address people's needs. We firmly believe and are committed to building up the global community to ensure that all peoples receive their proper due. That includes caring for our planet Earth which is home for all of us today and for our children tomorrow.

The more I worked with the United Nations, the more evident it was how close a fit there is between its overarching vision as set forth in the UN Charter, especially the Preamble, and our own aims as a religious congregation. We are committed to making the world a better place for all. Although religious congregations at the UN may be few and have very limited resources, we are a persistent voice challenging all member states to live up to the hopes that "We, the Peoples of the United Nations" expect of our governments. Our long-time commitment to live and work among and in solidarity with the vulnerable groups of our societies—people living in poverty, the excluded and minorities, children—makes us also aware of the importance of examining social and economic structures which are unjust and inequitable. This in my view is why we have made the investment to become NGOs accredited to the UN. Working to create a more just and humane world order is a moral imperative for all. Certainly, we can rejoice in this day that the Spirit has given the Church the leader Pope Francis who embodies this message so powerfully in gesture, as in word.

What I have just described I very much took for granted before coming to the work of advocacy at the UN. I now have a better grasp of the value these skills and perceptions could be for others working as advocates for vulnerable people whose voices are so often otherwise not present in policy discussions. As I have come to realize this on the intergovernmental level, I am beginning to see more clearly how this experience could also be directed on the local and national levels. These acquired skills and manner of working with others could have a great multiplier effect.

I have been struck by the number of government representatives at the United Nations in New York who asked us what our organizations were doing to build up the capacity of local NGOs in countries such as their own. In examining and reflecting on the new dimension of the SNDdeNs in their "identity" as an NGO, I now see that one of the great challenges facing international NGOs is to pass on these skills and experiences to our various constituents on the local and national levels so that we empower and build up the capacity of the people we are serving. They in turn can become more effectively organized as civil society groups who could contribute to the development of people-centered policies in their own localities and governments.

The work of our members the last two hundred years has for the most part been focused on direct services to people in their needs.

Today we are also being challenged in our experience of being a recognized NGO, to share with our local populations what they need to organize themselves as effective members of civil society. This requires that we consciously build up their confidence, skills, and conviction so that they can pressure their civic leaders to serve their people by a commitment to promote the common good. Together we can also develop and test programs of action which respective governments can adopt, expand, and replicate

As people grow in their skills to organize themselves, share their different perspectives, and trust their abilities, they will also have a greater capacity to join with one another in nongovernmental organizations committed to promoting the larger, common good of their local and national societies and ultimately their shared responsibility for the global common good. Confidence, commitment, and convictions are powerful tools for social change. As our members on the ground appropriate this new facet of their identity—especially our members who come from societies where civil society organizations are as yet very young—my hope is that they will see the possibility and their responsibility for building the capacity of local NGOs. I can appreciate this will be a slow process, remembering my own experience before being immersed in the NGO community at the UN. I hope that in the field we will come to see that our work in schools, dispensaries, and other institutions must empower those we serve to participate fully in the social development of their communities. In doing so in an open and collaborative way, the religious can model for both the people we serve and their governments the importance of recognizing and supporting local initiatives. Rather than working in a competitive or adversarial way, all of us will discover the power of partnerships based on mutual respect and reciprocity. Organizations such as ours for centuries have been working to realize what today are called the Millennium Development Goals, especially MDGs 1–7. We see that this is no longer enough; we must join forces with others so that the world community change the global structures which continue to make people poor and deprived of their basic human needs (MDG 8).

Social harmony is fostered when people feel that they are making a difference and are contributing to their societies. Welcoming all to the table, developing skills and attitudes too often neglected, and valuing voices too often silenced promote the kind of social inclusion that goes a long way toward reducing the pent-up frustrations caused by exclusion. Building these kinds of partnerships creates both a model and a kind of social integration that puts people at the center of development and enables them to craft and monitor social policy.

I have seen this in the collaboration and shared commitment to the larger common good by the members in the NGO Community at the UN. I am confident that our organizations can make much more of this experience by sharing it with our colleagues at the grassroots level. As has been evident in the recent years in the economic sphere, unfettered competition serves the small minority who end up on the top of the pile—not the majority who end up on the bottom. The resultant growing inequality and inequity of competitive systems is counterproductive to the good of the whole. The same is true of social systems. A major challenge today for nongovernmental organizations in the field of social development is to demonstrate that another way is possible. Over the years my conviction in the power of solidarity forged in a universal sisterhood/brotherhood has led me to see it as a force strong enough to pierce through the long-established but artificial barriers founded on national interest so that we can all claim as our own the common good of a global humanity.

I am now back in Africa working in the educational sphere in Kenya. I have as a consequence of my service at the UN new eyes, and I am still searching concretely how I can inspire those with whom I work and whom I serve to believe that we can together build more effective civil society organizations to effect change for our people. I am convinced we will do this most effectively when we work in tandem with those who are trying to address the structural issues of global injustice. I am still concerned in the day to day with plumbing, the vagaries of our electrical grid, and car mechanics. But I know that far more important than these are the longer term challenges of assuring that the basic needs of my brothers and sisters are what must engage me—hopefully, with them—for the very long time.

THE SIGNIFICANCE OF PLACE – UNITED NATIONS

Partnering Religious Congregations with UNICEF

Deirdre Mullan, RSM, PhD

> "Give me a place to stand, and I will move the world."
>
> —Archimedes

Christ! Gospel! People! A commitment to justice rooted in love! The women and men who serve as their community delegates to the United Nations are here as the voice and witness to the corporate stance that religious congregations have taken to be prophetic witnesses to justice. They believe, as the Greek mathematician Archimedes said, that given the right place, we could change the world!

Investing in a representative at the UN is a community's way of taking Catholic social teaching seriously and concretely. It is the community's radical commitment to Jesus's vision of the reign of God by working for ecological stewardship and social justice in solidarity with the poor and oppressed of our world, especially women and children.

Most of the men and women who represent their congregations here are people of the vision. They know that it is easier to critique the present than to create an alternative future—knowing that such a future is God's work! They come from very small and some larger congregations, and the vision that they bring to the United Nations is a quality of soul, which sees the presence of God in real life. They see the holy in the suffering of this world and feel compelled to work for a world where no one is excluded. At the United Nations, religious ask uncomfortable questions because they know firsthand the face of suffering, the feel of suffering, and the smell of suffering, and they are able to hone in on the lives of the excluded people of our planet. They speak up and speak out and are playing a significant role in shaping a more human world.

UNICEF, the children's wing of the United Nations, recognized this when they invited me to look at ways where they could form effective partnerships with religious on the ground. There are some very large and some very small religious congregations here. Some have formed partnerships. The latter could not be here nor have their voices heard if we were not partnering together, thus enabling all voices to have a place at the table. Their message is clear and direct because they recognize that consumerism is faceless; it is without conscience and is unrestrained by anything other than its own materialistic dynamics, and thus it is incapable of having moral responsibility.

Individually and collectively, the members and congregations who make up what we call RUN (Religious at the United Nations) passionately believe that together we can transform this behemoth called injustice by recognizing the right of every person to life in a safe environment and world *where all indeed will have enough.*

If we were ever to engage radically with the humanitarian and ethical vision of Jesus, it is at the United Nations or indeed with UNICEF, where the heartbeat of nations is monitored. It is here that governments meet as equals and are called to be moral agents with responsibility for the common good. We are here to make sure that government representatives and UN agencies are people of their word! As we face the future together, it is with the realization that we as a species have violated planetary boundaries, and we are left with the life and death question: *"Can there be progress at the cost of survival itself?"*

Speaking about the role of NGOs at the United Nations, Secretary-General Ban Ki-moon said, "Our times demand a new definition of cooperation—governments, the private sector, and civil society working together for the collective global good."[5] We are at a great moment of transformation; there is a sense that we are on the brink of a future that is at once known and unknown, linked to our present experience yet beyond and different from it.

Will we have the courage to grasp it? Or will we continue with business as usual, oblivious to the mayhem around us? Even among women and men religious, people are asking questions. Many of our community members cannot understand the point of having a representative at the United Nations, or they question the United Nations' lack of relevance in a world gone astray. Our members, who work day in and day out, on the ground with the poorest of the poor, see the United Nations as the greatest talk show in the world! And our members and critics have a point. If the collective good is indeed the focus of the UN, then the organization must urgently reform its structure in order to stay relevant in a world facing unprecedented conflicts. The UN's self-inflicted wounds have not done the organization any favors; yet, for all its indignities, the organization has helped colonized peoples in the developing world achieve their independence, causing UN membership to nearly quadruple from fifty-one to 193 member states since its founding. The UN is the embodiment of the "world's conscience" because it is the place where governments assemble to enshrine their legal and moral commitments. It is the home of international rules that, if followed, would breed greater peace and security. And yet for all its faults and failing, the UN and its children's agency—UNICEF—day in and day out provide food for 118 million people in seventy-five countries; vaccinates 40 percent of the world's children, saving two million lives each year; assists forty million refugees and others fleeing war, famine, and persecution; fights climate change; and leads international efforts in the wake of natural disasters.

Anthony Lake, Chief Executive Officer of UNIEF, recognizes the contribution of religious and often says, "Long before there was a UNICEF, women and men religious were on the ground meeting the needs of some of the world's poorest and most vulnerable children."

---

5   Speech at the World Economic Forum, Davos, Switzerland, January 29, 2009.

What inspires each of us is different and yet what keeps us focused is the vision of a world where no one is excluded, knowing that God has promised to be with us, to see things through with us ——to be the conscience of our world. Or as Irish poet Seamus Heaney says more eloquently in his poem "The Republic of Conscience":

> When I landed in the republic of conscience . . .
> The woman in customs asked me to declare
> the words of our traditional cures and charms
> to heal dumbness and avert the evil eye.
>
> No porters. No interpreter. No taxi.
> You carried your own burden and very soon
> your symptoms of creeping privilege disappeared . . .

Are we up to this challenge?

MULTILEVEL COMMUNITY WITNESSING

Augustinians International

John Paul Szura, OSA

Introduction

The Augustinians have officially established an association with the United Nations as a nongovernmental organization, opening to the Augustinian family a two-way dialogue relationship with the UN. By undertaking this UN ministry, as many other religiously inspired NGOs have done, the Augustinians have taken a significant step toward Second Vatican Council renewal. In accord with Vatican II's 1965 Pastoral Constitution on the Church in the Modern World, this UN ministry can bring us more deeply into "the joys and the hopes, the grief and the anxieties of this age." Also in accord with Vatican II renewal, this UN ministry can occasion a more faithful return to our original charism, particularly to a more fully authentic community life as was lived by St. Augustine himself.

UN NGO Ministry

It is well known that Church documents have consistently recognized the "indispensable" role of the United Nations in the modern world. In continuity with his predecessors, Pope Francis recently reiterated the Holy See's esteem and appreciation for the United Nations as an indispensable means of building an authentic family of peoples. The Holy See values the efforts of this distinguished institution "to ensure world peace, respect for human dignity, the protection of persons, especially the poorest and most vulnerable, and harmonious economic and social development" (Pietro Cardinal Parolin, Secretary of State on behalf of Pope Francis, addressing the 69th Session of the UN General Assembly September 29, 2014). However, just as consistent but far less known is the Church's recognition of the indispensable role of UN NGO ministry. In his October 2, 1979, New York address, Pope John Paul II explicitly acknowledges the need for this ministry and describes it as a two-way dialogue relationship: "No organization, however, not even the United Nations or any of its specialized agencies, can alone solve the global problems which are constantly brought to its attention if its concerns are not shared by all the people. It is then the privileged task of the nongovernmental organizations to help bring these concerns into the communities and the homes of the people and to bring back to the established agencies the priorities and aspirations of the people, so that all the solutions and projects which are envisaged may be truly geared to the needs of the human person . . ."

The pope's above description of the NGO two-way dialogical relationship with the UN corresponds to the two major types of NGOs—those associated with the Department of Public Information (DPI), communicating from the UN to the people; and those associated with the Economic and Social Council (ECOSOC), communicating from the people to the UN. The Augustinians now enjoy both DPI and ECOSOC association as a faith-based NGO.

Of course what is said of the UN NGO ministry applies to that of the Augustinians as well. But far beyond that, Augustine's life and works bear a profound affinity with the UN system as it impacts all levels of human life—local, national and world. The multilevel character of the UN system is anticipated by Augustine's observation, "Because every man [sic] is a neighbor to all men [sic], one should not allow any kind of distance where there is common human nature" (En. In ps. 118, 8, 2). This concise observation of Augustine expresses an ideal he constantly held and actively embraced: a life in community that is simultaneously local, national and world—a patristic foreshadowing of the magisterium's development that in the modern world the social question has reached worldwide importance without losing either local or national relevance.

Augustinian Spirituality: Living Multilevel Community

At the heart of Augustinian spirituality is life in common modeled after the ancient Christian community witnessed in the Acts of the Apostles (2:42 and 4:32–35). This ancient community was faithful to the apostles' teaching and the breaking of bread, they held all goods in common, and all members enjoyed fellowship of one heart and one mind in God. This even today characterizes the core values of the Augustinian charism that can be named simply as Truth, Unity, Love—*Veritas, Unitas, Caritas.*

This fundamental insight into the Augustinian charism is beyond controversy; whether it is practiced by vowed religious or by lay members or collaborators of the Augustinian family, it is faithful to the charism each in their own way. But particularly in our modern world and in response to calls for Church renewal, we would do well to return to Augustine's full understanding of community to retrieve his multilevel approach so as to put it into practice.

It has been noted that Jesus uses similar tripartite levels in his salvation narratives. Salvation has come to this house in the case of his visit to Zacchaeus and his household (Luke 19:9). Cities and nations are judged: "woe to you Charozin"; "woe to you Bethsaida" (Matthew 11:21). Consider also the last judgment narrative of Matthew 25:32–45 and the "great commission" (Matthew 28:19) to go to the whole world which lies at the heart of Vatican II. We would do well to accept the challenge of living in community on local, national, and world levels. For as Augustine said: "After the city or town is the world, cited by philosophers as the third level of human society. The philosophers start with the household, go on to the city and finally come upon the world. And just as it is with dangers of the sea, the bigger the community, the more trouble there is" (*City of God* 19:7).

The multilevel community aspect of Augustinian spirituality takes on a more urgent relevance in our present age as the social question takes on a truly worldwide character. Pope Paul VI brings this insight into explicit awareness in 1967: "Today it is most important for people to understand and appreciate that the social question ties all men together, in every part of the world. In the first place a possible misunderstanding has to be eliminated. Recognition that the 'social question' has assumed a worldwide dimension does not at all mean that it has lost its incisiveness or its national and local importance. On the contrary, it means that the problems in industrial enterprises or in the workers and union movements of a particular country or region are not to be considered as isolated cases with no connection. On the contrary, they depend more and more on the influence of factors beyond regional boundaries and national frontiers." This calls for the living out of the principles of solidarity as John Paul II emphasized in *Sollicitudo Rei Socialis*, 39, 40. Indeed, Augustine explicitly includes the world's entirety in an extended offer to all toward community.

Augustinian UN NGO Ministry: Empowering Multilevel Community

Living community on just one level is a daunting task for so many issues, so many complexities, and so many limitations bear upon us. Moreover, the level of "world" is especially challenging. Augustine in *City of God* 19:7 cited above uses the dangers of the vast sea as a metaphor to illustrate the grave scope of world problems. He then immediately warns us that if we do not overcome our world's diversity of languages so as to begin speaking with each other with real human communication, then real human neighborliness would be impossible in spite of our common human nature. Yet each level of community—local, national, world—does actually relate to the other two, and upon reflection, we can gain insight into their mutual interaction. Thus, living multilevel community is still our ideal and still even a practical reality to strive for.

This responsibility of multilevel community is precisely why the Augustinian UN NGO ministry with its two-way dialogical relationship is a providential blessing. This ministry has been established to empower Augustinians throughout the world to live more effectively on the world level as well as on the local and the national. Put in other words, it is true that the UN has enormous resources that can and do benefit us. Yet we are not at the UN only to take advantage of these resources. It is also true that the UN benefits greatly from its many associated NGOs. Yet we are not there simply for what we can do for the UN. Nor is UN NGO ministry a work done by others to whom we can transfer our world responsibilities and thus avoid dealing with them. On the contrary, it is through UN NGO ministry that we do whatever we do with, for, and in Church and world with more powerful apostolic and operational effectiveness. As asserted in the "Introduction" above, this UN ministry can occasion a more faithful return to our original charism, particularly to a more fully authentic community life as lived by St. Augustine himself.

Augustinian UN NGO Ministry: A Work In Progress

Consistent with John Paul II's words to NGOs cited above, it is the "privileged task" of the Augustinian UN NGO to maintain the two-way dialogue between the UN and the people. The UN is an enormous treasury of resources for all the earth's people in their homes, their cities, their countries, and their world. Through our NGO ministry, the UN can effectively speak with them. And the people themselves have much to say. Through our NGO ministry, they can effectively speak to the UN. The present state of this dialogue can be found on the Augustinian UN NGO website augustinians-un.org, a site that makes detailed examples here unnecessary. But we may note that conversation has begun with the World Tourism Organization (WTO) on human trafficking, with the United Nations International Strategy for Disaster Reduction (UNISDR) on disaster response, and with the World Food Program (WFP) on hunger. Conversation has begun with the offering of several of our projects to the world community as best practices, with some of our elementary schools using the UN's education resource CyberSchoolBus, with NGO collaboration in psychology, farming, and engineering. This two-way dialogue will take time to develop and mature. It is still a work in progress, but it is already well begun. May its good beginning be an invitation for all to participate. New York UN Headquarters is the on-site location of this UN NGO ministry and is under the leadership of our main representative, being at the time of this writing Rev. Emeka Obiezu, OSA, assisted by staff including volunteers. It is supported by an extended NGO team present in several countries. The activities of this ministry are guided by three priorities—education, development, human rights—terms chosen because of their relevance to Augustinian ministry worldwide, their honored and well understood meaning in international settings, and their correspondence to the Augustinian core values of Truth, Unity, Love.

WE ARE ONE HUMAN FAMILY, ONE EARTH COMMUNITY
Sisters of Charity Federation

Caroljean Willie, SC, PhD

The opening words of the Preamble to the Earth Charter provide an excellent introduction to our role on the global stage. It states: "We stand at a critical moment in Earth's history, a time when humanity must choose its future. As the world becomes increasingly interdependent and fragile, the future at once holds great peril and great promise. To move forward we must recognize that in the midst of a magnificent diversity of cultures and life-forms we are one human family and one earth community with a common destiny . . ."

As we look at our world today we realize that we live in very difficult times. It is easy to feel overwhelmed by the violence which surrounds us. Yet it is this world into which we are called to speak God's word, and it is our deeply held belief that we are one human family, one Earth community with a common destiny that both necessitates and gives meaning to our presence at the United Nations.

The late Nobel Laureate Ralph Bunche once said, "The United Nations exists not merely to preserve the peace but also to make change—even radical change—possible without violent upheaval. The United Nations has no vested interest in the status quo. It seeks a more secure world, a better world, a world of progress for all peoples.

In the dynamic world society which is the objective of the United Nations, all peoples must have equality and equal rights."

The UN, despite its many failings, is the one institution that seeks the common good of all humanity. Our time is now to be part of this global community and join with our brothers and sisters from every corner of the Earth to raise up a new vision of the world—a world where dignity and respect are accorded all members of the human family, a world where conflict is resolved through dialogue not destruction. We are at the United Nations because we know that God's kin-dom has no borders and that we are called to minister to the human family wherever there is a need.

The Sisters of Charity Federation represents twelve religious congregations whose 3,400 members work in twenty-seven countries throughout the world. Our federation is an official nongovernmental organization (NGO) at the United Nations. An NGO is defined as an international organization which has not been created by a formal agreement between governments. There are two levels of affiliation as NGOs at the United Nations. The first is affiliation through the Department of Public Information (DPI), which accounts for about 75 percent of all NGOs. The second are those in formal relationship with the Economic and Social Council (ECOSOC). Our federation has both DPI and ECOSOC status.

The shared charism of federation members, the love of Christ, urges us; and our common mission to serve those living in poverty impels us to work in multiple venues toward the eradication of poverty. At the United Nations we seek to evaluate UN and national policies according to the principles of Catholic social teaching and positions affirmed by the federation in order to support appropriate initiatives—thus influencing by presence, dialogue, interventions, and collaboration the political, economic, social, and humanitarian policies of the UN. The priority concerns of our membership are issues pertaining to the environment, poverty eradication, human trafficking, and migration.

Committee membership is the means through which we collaborate, prepare for yearly commissions, and lobby country missions to advocate on these issues. Our federation is represented on multiple committees by both the main and alternate representatives in New York as well as by congregational members who work in the greater New York area and can attend occasional committee meetings that connect to their ministries.

The federation NGO office provides the opportunity for members to participate in United Nations' orientation programs to learn more about how the organization works and how they can become more involved through disseminating information and through advocacy at the local level. It also affords members an opportunity to attend the Commission for Social Development, the Commission on the Status of Women, and the Permanent Forum on Indigenous Issues. When the Commission for Sustainable Development was operative, members also participated in that.

Yearly the NGO office hosts two to four interns for varying amounts of time. Members of the federation from India, South Korea, Belize, the United States, and Canada have served as interns. In addition the office makes internships available to youth working or going to school in the greater New York area. Interns from Syria, Myanmar, and the United States have taken advantage of this opportunity. The interns bring unique gifts to the office with their enthusiasm, desire to learn, and willingness to share the experiences gleaned through their studies and/or ministries. More than eight interns have offered to share their expertise with other NGOs through briefings. Topics have included: empowering women in India through self-help groups, working with trafficked women and youth, eradicating malaria through the use of herbs and Artemisia, and developing an awareness of and capacity building for the handicapped in Belize, among others.

In order to faithfully represent members at the United Nations, it is essential to know what is happening on the ground. Approximately one-third of the main representative's time is spent visiting member congregations at local levels and offering workshops on the role of the federation at the UN, on climate change, on advocacy, and on systemic change, among others. These on-site visits also provide the opportunity to see the on-the-ground initiatives in which members are engaged and to make connections among members who are engaged in similar endeavors as well as use the concrete information obtained as the basis for written interventions for commissions and lobbying efforts at the UN. Yearly the federation sponsors side events at the commissions in order to demonstrate best practices.

As members of the Sisters of Charity Federation, we are also a part of the larger worldwide Vincentian family. This includes men and women, religious and laity, whose congregations or organizations trace their roots to St. Vincent de Paul (1581–1660) who was renowned for his compassion, humility, and generosity, as well as for his innovative work among those living in poverty. The Vincentian family includes almost two million members working in more than 150 countries. As an international family, we have committed ourselves to working on systemic change. To this end workshops have been held in Asia, Africa, South, Central, and North America, and in several locations in Europe. The primary purpose of these workshops is to educate members about the nature of systemic change and to give them a new lens through which to view their ministries to address the root causes of poverty. In addition to the workshops at country levels, regional workshops are now engaging people at more local levels, both members of the Vincentian family as well as those with whom and to whom they minister.

Participants in these workshops are challenged to look at the systems of which their individual ministries are a part and to begin to identify the elements that influence the lives of people within the system—family, institutions, jobs, housing, food and drink, health care, education, moral values, spiritual development, etc. When all of the elements in a system function together positively, people thrive; if one or several of these elements are lacking, the whole system breaks down.

This emphasis on systemic change flows into and out of our work at the United Nations. The problems confronting the world community today are systemic problems. Unless and until they are recognized as such, international interventions offer nothing more than Band-Aid solutions to poverty, conflict, and environmental degradation. We believe that systemic change responds promptly to human needs while respecting the individual's right to determine his/her own future. As this world body moves from an emphasis on the Millennium Development Goals (MDGs) to Sustainable Development Goals (SDGs) it has become increasingly more aware of the need to engage people at all levels of society in the development process. Rather than create goals *for* people, the SDGs seek to create goals *with* people.

As the Sisters of Charity Federation collaborates with other members of the Vincentian family to look at the root causes of poverty and conflict throughout the world and to engage in changing those systems which continually oppress people, they have gained insights and created tools which they bring to their work on committees and in other venues at the UN. These include but are not limited to

1. involving those living in poverty themselves, including the young and women at all stages in the identification of needs, planning, implementation, evaluation, and revision as essential to development;
2. having a holistic vision addressing a series of basic human needs—individual and social, spiritual and physical, especially needs such as jobs, health care, housing, education, and spiritual growth;
3. placing particular emphasis on self-help and self-sustaining programs;
4. fostering transparency by inviting participation in preparing budgets and in commenting on financial reports, while promoting good money management and maintaining careful controls over the use of assets; and
5. constructing a shared vision with diverse stakeholders— poor communities, interested individuals, donors, churches, governments, NGOs, the private sector, unions, and the media.

There are times when we voice the concerns of those living in poverty at the UN, but more often we strive to bring those living in poverty to speak for themselves because we truly believe that "the vantage point of marginal people is a privileged place of encounter with God."[6] The ability to speak at the UN empowers people and tells them that their lives matter. We can and do gather data that can be used by policy makers. We can and do raise our voices on behalf of those who live in poverty, but their voices bring reality and

---

[6] Sr. Patricia Farrell, "Navigating the Shifts," Presidential Address, LCWR Assembly 2012.

authenticity to the table. Their presence in front of world leaders puts a human face on the cost of failed policies and inaction.

The goal of systemic change in the mission of the Sisters of Charity Federation and the larger Vincentian family to create a more just world order parallels the purpose of the United Nations as expressed in Article 1 of the United Nations Charter: "to maintain international peace and security . . . to develop friendly relations among nations based on respect for the principle of equal rights and self-determination . . . to achieve international cooperation in solving international problems of an economic, social, cultural, or humanitarian character . . . and to be a center for harmonizing the actions of nations in the attainment of these common ends."

Pablo Casals once said, "The love of one's country is a splendid thing. But why should love stop at the border?" We are at the United Nations because we know that God's kin-dom has no borders and that wherever there is suffering and pain we are called to be present. The UN offers us the opportunity to work collaboratively with people throughout the world to foster an understanding of the realities of our brothers and sisters everywhere and to find ways of working together to build a just and equitable society for all. In the words of former UN Secretary-General Kofi Annan, "More than ever before in human history, we share a common destiny. We can master it only if we face it together. And that, my friends, is why we have the United Nations."

The vision statement of the Sisters of Charity Federation is: "Impelled by the Gospel charism of Charity, we commit ourselves to be in solidarity with our sisters and brothers who are poor and marginalized. We will use the energy of our love, the gifts and talents of the members of our communities, and our material and spiritual resources to collaborate in the creation of systemic change locally and globally for the common good of all." That is why the Sisters of Charity Federation is committed to ministry at the United Nations.

PASSION FOR JESUS, PASSION FOR LIFE

Enter the Passionists in the Heart of Politics

Kevin Dance, CP

I was born into a world and baptized into a church that reeked of tradition and stability. I was ordained into a church whose foundations were being rocked by the Spirit-driven Vatican Council. I have ministered in a world that is convulsing with change where tradition and stability are daily challenged.

The Church's self-understanding has changed as the world has changed. We have often buried our heads in the sand to avoid the pain of change. But the Second Vatican Council called our religious communities to recover and rediscover their *raison d'être* by absorbing anew the spirit of our founders and by learning how to read "the signs of the times."[7] These changes have given us a whole new vocabulary. So now we speak of systemic change, social structures, social sin, and of how doing justice is "constitutive of the gospel."

---

[7]   "Decree on the Up-to-Date Renewal of Religious Life: Perfectae Caritatis, #2," ed. Austin Flannery, vol. 1 of *Vatican Council II: The Conciliar and Post Conciliar Documents New Revised Edition* (Northport, New York: Costello Publishing Company, 2004), 612.

Our modern world—with all its discoveries, inventions, and positive developments—is wonderful to see. But is has a dirty underbelly. Forced displacement of millions of peoples, with violence done to children and women and trafficking in human persons as sexual or cheap units of work are contemporary forms of slavery. The untold suffering caused by this violence is shaping a world that is more fractured, bleeding, and vulnerable than ever before. Economic growth, the removal of effective regulation of the financial markets, and placing profit before people widens the inequality gap and wreaks havoc in the lives of billions of people. Add to this the ever-increasing threat to the survival of the physical environment, and we have a world crying out for daily acts of service and practical love. It cries to heaven for people who will speak a word where change is possible.

It Is Good for Us to Be Here

Kofi Annan, former Secretary General of the United Nations[8] indicated how important he saw the presence of people of faith if the UN is to be effective.

> Men and women of faith are crucial to the United Nations. As teachers and guides, *you can be agents of change* and inspire people to new levels of public service. You can help bridge the chasms of ignorance, fear, and misunderstanding that plague our world. You can set an example of interfaith dialogue, cooperation, and respect. My great predecessor Dag Hammarskjöld once said [and I quote]: "The United Nations stands outside—necessarily outside—all confessions. But it is, nevertheless, an instrument of faith. As such, it is inspired by what unites, and not by what divides the great religions of the world."

---

[8]   Kofi Annan (remarks at the Holy Family Church, September 2006), http://www.un.org/sg/statements/?nid=2198

Enter the Passionists: Passion in the Heart of Politics

As millions of people made their way to Rome to celebrate the Holy Year 2000, Passionists celebrated the year by meeting in general chapter in Brazil, a country of great wealth and horrifying poverty and injustice. It was the first time our congregation had celebrated the "ecclesial event" of a general chapter outside Rome. Our theme was "The Passion of Jesus: Passion for Life."[9]

Many things excited me at that meeting in Itaici, Brazil, in the Holy Year 2000. The call "to justice and peace and the integrity of creation" was firmly on the agenda. We reminded ourselves that we, vowed Passionists, do not *own* the Passionist charism. It is God's gift which we share with many others who've also been drawn into it. My heart beat a little faster as we agreed that working for justice is no optional extra, but it lies at the heart of our charism and spirituality. Jesus, in his own body on the Cross, tore down the walls separating us from one another, from our God, and from the glorious creation in which we live out our lives. The icing on the cake for me was the chapter's decision to search for new places in which to speak the Gospel of the Passion. As part of this we would seek to link the Passionist family with the United Nations—the only truly multilateral policy-making body in the world.

Faithful to the call of the church and to the road map of the chapter, Passionists reaffirmed our commitment to justice.

> In a world where increasing numbers of poor people are being "crucified" by unjust political and economic structures, our sense of solidarity calls us to proclaim the Gospel of Justice and Peace. Justice is an essential part of the Gospel.
>
> A proper sense of solidarity also requires us to take a stand alongside those who defend the integrity of

---

[9]   General Curia, Roma, 44th General Chapter of the Congregation of the Passion of Jesus, Itaici, Brazil, October 2000

creation, for we know that "all creation groans in birth pangs" (Rom. 8, 22). It calls us to promote a holistic view of life, aware of the interdependence of its many elements, spiritual, political, social, economic, and environmental. We hold a passion for life in all its richness, diversity, plurality, and fragility.[10]

I later learned that I would be the one asked to go to New York to begin this work for our Passionist family. I arrived in New York on a bleak winter day two weeks before Christmas and twelve weeks after the barbaric act by which two planes filled with captive people were flown into the tallest buildings in New York, the World Trade Center. The city was stunned into silence. In this context I began my ministry . . . It seemed that nothing I had done so far in my life prepared me for the work I was to do at the United Nations. Later I saw that everything I had been involved in up to now was a building block in creating what has become Passionists International, our nongovernmental organization.

The World Sets the Agenda and We Respond

Without warning, the stable democracy of Kenya erupts in violence. A tidal wave of financial instability, issuing from the greed of US financial institutions, washes round the world. The collective punishment of the Palestinian people in Gaza threatens peace in the Middle East. Passionists are present in each of these places. Change, turbulence, and uncertainty are the shape of life today. How do we bring the hope and healing, central to the Passionist charism, to the pain and division of our world? In a globalized world, rugged individualism is finished! We either learn to walk together and to work together, or we perish together. We are joined at the hip!

At Passionists International, by speaking the word of the Cross into the policy discussions at the UN, we aim to be the other arm to complement the efforts "back home" of our Passionist brothers and sisters to share the transforming power of the Cross by their

---

[10] Congregation of the Passion of Jesus Christ, 44th General Chapter, Itaici, Sao Paulo, Brazil, 2000, No. 4.6

daily love and service. If our work at the UN is to be effective, our different ministries—local and global—must inform and strengthen each other in radiating Christ's love to a complex, troubled, and pain-filled world.

> His Passion and death are no mere historical events. They are ever-present realities to people in the world of today, "crucified" as they are by injustice, by the lack of a deep respect for human life, and by a hungry yearning for peace, truth, and the fullness of human existence. (Passionist Constitution #65)[11]

I shared this story in a workshop with our general council, after nine years of experience at the UN:

> At the multi-faith consultation on the Millennium Development Goals (MDGs), a lovely, gracious Palestinian woman, Ms. Doris Salah, in introducing me to a young woman, said: "This is Father Kevin. He is a Passionist. Until I met him, I thought the Passionists did nothing but pray. I didn't know that they were interested in justice and such things. I had two cousins who were Passionists in Jerusalem."

> This was a sobering comment. It is my conviction that we are at the UN to effect systemic change. The UN is far from perfect. But it is the only forum where all countries are present to seek solutions to global problems. NGOs speak for "the people." We aim to bring our experience, strengthened by analysis and prayerful reflection, to the international negotiating table by giving a voice to those who are voiceless.[12]

---

[11] "Passionist Constitution," http://www.passionist.org/files/Passionist%20 Rule%20and%20Constitutions.pdf

[12] "Vision for Passionist presence to the UN: Workshop with General Council," August 2011

So by becoming an NGO that advocates with the governments of the world, we want to let the voices of our poor and excluded brothers and sisters be heard. The UN is far from perfect, but it is the only forum open to all peoples to work for a more just, humane, and peaceful world. In 2000, our general chapter in Brazil saw the need to announce the Gospel of Life in new places and new ways. The United Nations was seen as one such Areopagus or marketplace calling for our prophetic presence. Father Ottaviano D'Egidio, in presenting the chapter document, reminded us that "[l]ooking upon our Crucified and Resurrected Lord, we cannot turn our backs on the struggle against the powers of evil, which offend and destroy man and conspire against human dignity as well as the dignity and beauty of all creation. Humanity's Calvary is likewise God's Calvary and constitutes the outermost frontier where *we are bound to be present*."

What We Do

Passionists International works on varied issues of concern, such as

1. the rights of indigenous peoples and the negative impact of extractive industries on their environment, health and human rights. A major success was playing an active role that saw the General Assembly adopt the United Nations Declaration on the Rights of Indigenous Peoples in the face of fierce resistance from some of the rich countries.
2. the promotion of policies of social inclusion that enable people forced to live in poverty be included in the life of their own society; describing them as "the poor" depersonalizes them and turns them into a problem to be solved. We religious NGOs managed to have these sisters and brothers of ours referred to in official UN documents as "poor people" or better still, "people living in poverty."
3. the advocacy for a universal policy of a Social Protection Floor in every country to protect the minimum health, education, and employment needs of every person.
4. the advocacy for a development model that is people centered and not primarily geared to uncontrolled economic

development focused on profit at the expense of the welfare and dignity of workers and people at the margins of life, undertaken with other NGOs to the policy makers. This includes exposing the massive amounts that corporations fail to contribute through tax avoidance and evasion.

How We Do It

To be effective at the UN we cannot work in isolation but must work in partnership. This involves close cooperation with other NGOs, with religious congregations, and with sympathetic governments. This is supported by the work of our members at the grassroots level. Any commitment to work for systemic change at the international level must link closely with our Passionist sisters and brothers' work for the most excluded people "on the ground." Their love and service give credibility to those of us who work in world fora such as the United Nations.[13]

How Our UN Passionist Presence Is Perceived

During the World Summit on Sustainable Development in Johannesburg, South Africa, in 2002, a young man interning in the UN Secretary General's office was intrigued to learn that we, a group of religious, wanted to take part in the decision making of the UN. The next day I received an e-mail from him, and the correspondence has continued. He sees our action as a small sign of hope. Faith groups and religious have some responsibility to keep the issues of ethics and values as part of the agenda of the UN.

The longer I was at the UN and perhaps learned a few ways to try to make a difference, the more I became convinced of the power and the potential for healing and transformation that lie at the heart of the crucified love of Christ broken open for *all* of us. I am sure that if the UN were emptied out of NGOs, poor countries would be worse off than they are. NGOs are the ones who consistently try to bring values and ethical discussions into the arena. As I said

---

[13]   Australian Passionist Province, *Holy Cross Newsletter* (2003)

earlier, our world cries out for daily acts of service and practical love. So many of our fellow religious around the world provide this with generous hearts. But our world also cries to heaven for people who will speak a word where change is possible. I treasure having been given the chance to speak just a few of those words.

UNANIMA:
Bringing the "Feminine Soul" to the UN

Michele Morek, OSU

We are the women of UNANIMA International—a coalition of nineteen congregations of women religious representing together about twenty thousand women all over the world. The coalition was named after the *UN* and *anima* (the Latin word for the feminine soul or life principle). UNANIMA does bring the energy of the feminine spirit to our work at the UN and, through our member communities, to over eighty countries around the world. In the rich experience of coming together in a common ministry—not just in one community, but in nineteen!—we manifest the one-ness to which the Gospel calls us.

Our member communities are the following:

- Carmelite Sisters of Charity, Vedruna
- Congregation of Bon Secours of Paris
- Congrégation of Notre Dame of Montreal
- Congregation of Our Lady of Sion
- Congregation of Sisters of Saint Agnes
- Daughters of Wisdom
- Handmaids of the Sacred Heart of Jesus
- Holy Union Sisters

- Missionary Sisters of the Sacred Heart (Cabrini Sisters)
- Religious of Jesus and Mary
- Sisters of Saint Brigid (Brigidine)
- Sisters of the Divine Savior (Salvatorian Sisters)
- Sisters of Providence
- Sisters of Saint Anne
- Sisters of the Holy Names of Jesus and Mary
- Society of the Holy Child Jesus
- Sœurs de l'Assomption de Sainte Vierge
- Religious Sisters of Charity (Ireland and Australia)
- Ursuline Sisters of Mount Saint Joseph

We joined together to expand our global outreach, to address world problems at the systemic level, and to collaborate on international issues of common concern. Our unique charisms enrich the work of UNANIMA through the educational, hospital, parish ministry, social justice, and other specialized work of our members. And our work together in UNANIMA brings a rich sense of global involvement, of being one with our brothers and sisters all over the world. In our work at the UN we are enriched by being more closely connected to the tragedies and triumphs of other nations, and we bring them to our prayer in new ways. We find new answers to Jesus's question "Who is your neighbor?" by expanding our vision in new ways to the whole world.

UNANIMA International (UI) works with the United Nations on issues relating to UI's special focus areas: women and children (especially those living in poverty, or who have been trafficked); immigrants and refugees; and the environment (especially water and climate change). UI is governed by a board consisting of one representative from each of the member congregations. The coalition coordinator and her assistant connect with the board, the leadership of the nineteen communities, and with regional coordinators who form other relational networks. They carry forward the UI vision through internet, phone, and personal visits. The work of UI, supported entirely by the contributions of the member congregations, includes the following:

1. *Lobbying*: UI takes issues to the United Nations by working on NGO committees; by offering its own written and oral interventions to UN working bodies; by directly talking with individual UN countries and departments; by offering educational events that bring its own congregations' "grassroots knowledge" to the UN; and by giving its membership the tools to work with UN agencies in their own countries. The goal of all these activities is to affect UN policies in the areas of UNANIMA's mission.

2. *Membership Education*: UI educates the membership of its congregations by offering them paid internships; by providing UN passes for members attending UN events; by publishing a monthly e-newsletter (in four languages) with news from the UN and from other member communities; by maintaining a website and Facebook page; and by providing educational activities for members of the board. The coordinator and board members also speak about UI and the United Nations at congregational events or to various other religious/civic groups.

3. *Education Projects/Activities*: UI has produced educational material on human trafficking and on water and had given workshops/lectures on various subjects across the United States and in several other countries. The UI human trafficking educational material is spread all over the world! Most recently, a two-year program in Kenya focused on "youth teaching youth," training a group of Catholic youth to go out to several parishes in the Nairobi area to train other youth in how to recognize and combat human trafficking. In 2013 a UI international youth workshop in northern Ghana attracted seventy-five youth, sisters from six UNANIMA communities, and other religious, clerical, and lay people working against trafficking in eight countries.

4. *Membership Networking / Ministry Support*: UI seeks to provide members with tools they need to work on issues of concern at their own country/regional/local level by sharing website connections, PowerPoint presentations, and the like. Currently UI is working on a pilot regional network project to connect UI sisters with each other, so they can share

resources and common concerns. Many individual sisters report back to UI that they have become involved with issues in their own countries, using resources provided by UI or shared by other UI member communities.

5. *Member Outreach*: Inspired by their experience with UNANIMA, many sisters take UI issues back to their own countries. In the last three years, board members have given anti-trafficking workshops for religious leaders in Ethiopia and have alerted groups of women religious leaders in Ireland to the issues of human trafficking and water pollution from fracking. Staff members and former interns have joined groups working against trafficking, those involved with water issues, or other social justice movements in the Philippines, South America, Australia, and the USA. An Australian member of parliament came to interview the UI staff on trafficking, migration, and other issues, saying, "The sisters sent me."

6. *Networking*: UI maintains a network of relationships with organizations all over the world, such as the Bakhita Initiative—a project of the US Catholic Sisters Against Human Trafficking (USCSAHT) named after Saint Bakhita, the patroness of trafficked persons. We are a parallel organization with Australian Catholic Religious Against Trafficking in Humans (ACRATH), Comité D'Action Contre La Traite Humaine Interne Et Internationale (CATHII) in Canada, and the Asian Pacific Women Religious Against Trafficking in Humans (APWRATH). APWRATH has now become part of Talitha Kum, an international organization of religious women against human trafficking, sponsored by the Union of International Superiors General (UISG). Recently the first steps have been taken to encourage the formation of networks of UNANIMA communities in different regions of the world. The sisters from our nineteen member communities are actively engaged in many religious ministry and social justice activities, and joining their voices together—all twenty thousand of them—will surely make them heard.

Challenges: The challenges are many. Working with a small staff on issues that are too complex for whole nations to solve, coping with the huge and confusing bureaucracy that is the UN reality, and having to be satisfied sometimes with tiny victories like the change of one word in a large document . . . these are the everyday realities of religious NGOs at the United Nations.

But women religious are uniquely qualified to collaborate with each other and with other groups, and the feminine gift of oneness as practiced in the coalition structure of UNANIMA embodies its charism of "One Spirit, One Mission, One Hope." We are transformed by the same Spirit which at Pentecost united a diverse band of disciples into a powerful group that would speak with one voice all over the world; dedicated to our common mission to minister to all people, especially the most vulnerable; and united in one hope that the message of the Gospel ultimately will transform the world. As we work toward this transformation, we and the other religious NGOs bring to the UN a vocal testimony to the oneness which is at the heart of the mission of the United Nations itself.

HEALING PRESENCE OF JESUS IN THE WOUNDED WORLD
Medical Mission Sisters

Celine Paramundayil MMS

We, the Medical Mission Sisters (MMS), are a nonprofit organization of women religious from twenty nationalities serving in five continents. Both canonical and associate members have a special focus on women and girls. Our caring, healing presence extends from the micro to the macro, from the grassroots to the United Nations for a better life for all. Involvement at the UN is an extension of the healing mission of Medical Mission Sisters who believe that care for the earth is integral to human health and wellbeing. We promote justice and peace by addressing systemic issues and human rights for sustainable development. We reach out to the victims of systemic injustice and those living in poverty as God's beloved children, and we are committed to care for them as well as the planet which is wounded and abused. The UN is the only place where the global issues are discussed and policies are made which impact particularly the lives of those living in poverty. This UN ministry is important for MMS to raise our voices on behalf of voiceless people and the planet because we believe that the community of life deserves a right to exist and flourish for the glory of God.

MMS and the United Nations

In 1992 Sr. Janet Gottschalk attended the UN Conference on Environment and Development (UNCED) held in Rio de Janeiro, Brazil. Sharing her experiences and reflections of that historic Earth Summit and the possible implications for MMS mission afterward, she named in particular Agenda 21, a comprehensive global action plan for sustainable development and a few other challenges, including the need for NGOs to be involved with the UN.

Many important issues such as poverty, population, indigenous people, land rights, debt, and structural adjustments were missing from the conversations. Health, healing, and wholeness were just not included. The MMS General Assembly noted that MMS in all sectors are already involved in many of the justice and environmental issues raised by the Earth Summit. Our chapter documents talk about how we are "interwoven in the total web of life." We are fully involved in our local situation, and we shy away from involvement at a macro level because it is too overwhelming. We recognized that our involvement in justice and ecological issues is an expression of our commitment and that it is important that we document and communicate that engagement among ourselves. The need to establish international linkages and networks was also recognized.

In 1993, the MMS decided to apply for special consultative status to the UN Economic and Social Council (ECOSOC) and accreditation with the UN Department of Public Information (DPI). In 1994, we received accreditation to DPI, and in 2000, were affiliated to ECOSOC. In 2000, Philo Morris MMS was appointed as the full time Main UN Representative, while Janet Gottschalk MMS and Theresita Hinnigan MMS continue to be the North American representatives to the UN. In 2010, Celine Paramundayil MMS became the main representative. We were accredited to the United Nations Framework Convention on Climate Change (UNFCCC) in 2011.

A couple of challenges are endured in this mission. As is the case with my own experience, many of those who represent their groups have no formal preparation for the job. They accept the appointment as a response to the congregation's need. As a result, their first encounter with the overwhelming UN vocabularies, structures, and meetings could be intimidating. Many have found comfort in the monthly meetings of cheerful and warm women and men representatives of religious from around the world at the UN.

MMS leadership continues to encourage members in all five continents to participate in regional and national meetings prior to major UN conferences as they are the places where contributions from local realities can be made. Advocacy at the national level is as important as advocacy at the international level since implementation has to happen at the country level.

The experiences of the past three years at the UN have helped me to connect the dots with the values of the Gospels, the MMS constitution, and the UN Charter. The opening paragraph of *Pacem in Terris* ("Peace on Earth"), the encyclical of Pope John XXIII, talks about "*[p]eace on earth, which all men of every era have most eagerly yearned for, can be firmly established only if the order laid down by God be dutifully observed.*" The current socioeconomic and environmental realities force us to work for a just world for all. Since 1945 the UN, an international organization, stands for peace and works for peace. We are happy to collaborate with the UN and to be a link with the people on the ground. We use every possible opportunity at the UN to raise the issues affecting people who live in poverty through written and oral interventions, organizing parallel events, as well as advocacy and lobbying with policy makers. We are connected to our membership through regular newsletters, e-mails, website, and Facebook. Through this information sharing connection, we provide them with UN information while they in turn inform us of what is happening on the ground.

For the first time in the history of the UN, an official session was conducted in 2013 to listen to the people living in extreme poverty. It was in the context of one of the proposed themes in the Secretary-General's High-level Panel Report for the post-2015 sustainable development agenda, "Leave no one behind." During the meeting one of the panelists, Juan Carlos from Ecuador said, "I don't like to be called poor, I don't want to be poor anymore," and he burst into tears. The shame attached to poverty was too much for him and the millions like him to bear. This incident touched my heart deeply and I told him after the meeting, "Juan, you are not poor. You have the skill and knowledge and you have something to contribute to the world." And I saw the glow on his face!

A few disturbing questions are: Why is the society attaching shame to the impoverished people of the world and not to those greedy extremely rich who grab the wealth which rightfully do not belong to them? Why are people who cause little to climate change suffering disproportionately for its effect, while the rich world which disproportionately contributed to it are not willing to change their unsustainable life style? Climate change is not only an environmental issue; it is a moral issue in which all people of God must get involved. As people of faith, we need to network nationally as well as internationally, not only for a change in policy but also for a change in mindset because that leads to structural change. Networking at the UN is the beauty of our involvement. The goal is to have a life of dignity for all human beings who are created in the image of God in solidarity with the community of life, the beautiful creation of God.

> "Alone we can do so little; together we can do
> so much." (Helen Keller)

Let us forge ahead joining hands and hearts! Together we can make a difference!

ESTABLISHING JUSTICE THAT IS EFFECTIVE IN TODAY'S WORLD

Maryknoll Sisters at the United Nations

Elizabeth Zwareva, MM

Maryknoll's mission at the United Nations is in accord with the aims and the underlying principles of the Earth Charter, "an international declaration of fundamental values and principles considered useful by its supporters for building a just, sustainable, and peaceful global society."

In a similar manner, our mission in the field has constantly sought to articulate the principles of "(1) respect[ing] Earth and life in all its diversity; (2) car[ing] for the community of life with understanding, compassion, and love; (3) [helping] build democratic societies that are just, participatory, sustainable and peaceful; and (4) secur[ing] Earth's bounty and beauty for present and future generations" (The Earth Charter, http://www.earthcharterinaction.org/content/pages/Read-the-Charter.html). It is now up to us to work together to make our world a happier, safer legacy for present and future generations.

Our responsibility as bearers of God's love and teachings, especially for the downtrodden, includes providing for immediate needs of others while also committing ourselves to social justice in society in which we live and work and worship. Both charity and justice are needed to accomplish this, to establish justice that is effective in today's world.

Our living witness to the existence of injustices, extreme poverty, disease, and violence is urgently needed in the UN debates that tend to lean toward political interests while forgetting to place people at the center of the debate. As a nongovernment organization at the UN, Maryknoll works to influence the UN agenda for the good of all by expressing the voice of those struggling to bring change into a world ravaged by social unrest, violence, disease, poverty, and war. Through open dialogue with other groups at the UN, our voice is demanding that nations work to promote peace and security in parts of the world where citizens, especially women and children, become victims of conflict. The Maryknoll Sisters' UN presence began in the 1970s as an accredited nongovernment organization.

As an indispensable ministry within the UN system, the significance of our witness is captured in this experience of one of our sisters. "At first I never dreamed that I would be doing the work, but here I am doing it because I have redefined my perspective of mission to include working with those who draft policies that affect what we do in the missions. This perspective took hold of me when I was still in mission. I saw it at the educational level and in a special way with those who chart the future through scientific research. At the UN, the same thing happens as we confront a world that is driven by greed and increase in inequalities. While the Millennium Development Goals have improved lives, they are yet to be redefined within the post–2015 development agenda.[14] It is great to fulfill goals, but how deep is the effect of fulfilling these goals for some while excluding others?"

Maryknoll continues to focus on issues that affect women and children, and a relationship with UNICEF has brought about important achievements. Among these was to create a Children's Rights Caucus in the preparation process toward the Social Summit.

---

[14] At the time of publication of this booklet, the UN has adopted the Sustainable Development Goals (SDGs) as part of the Post 2015 development agenda. This new agenda will set the world's development priorities from 2016 to 2030.

Another success was to publish information the public needs to observe in armed conflict to protect children.

An important aspect of Maryknoll's work is linking the global and the local. To realize this we sponsor fieldworkers to attend UN events. With such opportunity the negative cultural practices against women and children such as the discrimination against Native American women and children are given a global perspective. When Maryknoll's UN mission accepted the challenges to address the issues of apartheid and women's rights, it helped a Maryknoller working in Africa to shift from a narrowly African focus to a wider world focus. As she once testified she now sees the world of advocacy as one loving, caring community dedicated to human rights. The same spirit of interconnectedness motivates Maryknoll's participation in world and UN Conferences on women including the conference and NGO forum in Beijing.

During some of the UN conferences we invite speakers from countries where we work, thus providing them the opportunity to speak for themselves at the events. This is a significant witness to Maryknoll's goal of ensuring that those directly affected at the local level are brought closer to the center. A human rights lawyer from Peru gave testimony at the UN on the impact of mining on a particular town in Peru, while a farmer from Mexico gave testimony at the UN.

At the UN, Maryknoll has paid particular attention to issues of financing for development (FfD), disarmament (nuclear and small arms concern), climate change (global warming and climate change), and sustainable development (concerns about maintaining progress while preserving the Earth). To realize its commitment to the Earth Charter, Maryknoll Sisters Congregation dedicated part of their property to earth's preservation through land conservation easements.

This UN presence is of mutual benefit to ourselves, the UN, and those we both serve, hoping to bring a more peaceful and sustainable world for all. The UN mission has encouraged a greater collaboration among the Maryknoll family. Our UN office is now a collaborative project of the Maryknoll Sisters, the Maryknoll Society (Fathers and Brothers), and the Maryknoll Lay Missioners, and it is part of the Maryknoll Office for Global Concerns in Washington, DC.

Maryknoll's spirit reflects an approach to mission by going to the edges "beyond Church circles" with the good news of the Gospel. Our bimonthly publication, *Maryknoll News Notes*, can be accessed at www.maryknollogc.org.

WORKING FOR JUSTICE, ACTING FOR PEACE

Loretto Community's Global Advocacy at the UN

Sally Dunne, Comember

The Loretto Community nongovernmental organization began its presence at the United Nations in 1991, to promote its values and advocate for issues on the international level by leveraging the insight and voices of those working at the grassroots level. Loretto has a long history of working for peace and justice in the United States and all over the world.

The Loretto Community is a congregation of Catholic vowed sisters and lay comembers who, individually and collectively, carry out the Community's mission: working for justice and acting for peace. The Community's origin is the Sisters of Loretto, who began on the Kentucky frontier in 1812, making Loretto one of the first religious communities of women founded in the United States. Loretto's founders—Mary Rhodes, Ann Havern, and Christina Stuart—responding to the need for education of the children in the area, decided to form a spiritual, religious community and to dedicate themselves to provide the education children living on the frontier so desperately needed. They experienced joy and meaning in their work and life together, and from this humble beginning in rural Kentucky, Sisters of Loretto subsequently opened over 225 schools across the United States. Loretto also spread its mission to China, Bolivia, Peru, Ghana, and Pakistan, among other places. The courage, concern, and energy of the Sisters of Loretto, nourished by the Gospel and communal love, remain with the Community as a lasting gift of hope.

Through the teachings and insights of Vatican II, the Loretto Community gained a new understanding of its mission. While still traditionally a teaching order, Loretto expanded its work into many fields to promote peace and justice, including healthcare, elder care, environmental stewardship, and advocacy. Just as frontier living shaped the lives of the early sisters, so a global society shapes contemporary Loretto. Much of the work of the Sisters of Loretto throughout the years has directly served people in need, but members of the Loretto Community have also been outspoken about social justice issues and have marched, protested, and advocated for systemic change in the areas of peace and disarmament; civil, labor, and human rights; women's empowerment and environmental justice. The sisters and comembers of Loretto currently continue to serve throughout the United States, in addition to its missions and partnerships in Pakistan, Ghana, and Guatemala.

As recognition grew that key concerns and commitments of the Loretto Community—such as working for peace and justice, women's issues, and solidarity with the world's poor—coincide with overarching aims of the United Nations, interest in attending meetings and participating in UN events grew as well. At the Loretto Assembly in 1991, suggesting that wider religious input and increased numbers of participants could have a significant impact on the UN and its deliberations, Mary Luke Tobin, SL moved a proposal that the Loretto Community establish nongovernmental organization (NGO) status at the United Nations and seek formal UN accreditation.

At the United Nations, the Loretto Community has engaged in a wide variety of issue-based committees with other NGO partners. This work allows Loretto to collaborate in our efforts to address challenges like disarmament, poverty eradication and reducing inequalities, financing for development, protecting the rights of migrants, empowering women and girls, and pursuing development that builds sustainable communities and nurtures and protects the Earth's resources. In addition to the day-to-day work on these issues,

Loretto also participates in larger collaborations with the wider UN system and has been present at many historic events like the World Conferences on Women and the UN Earth Summit in Rio de Janeiro.

Today, the Loretto Community NGO works in the same spirit as the early sisters, committed to improving the conditions of those who suffer from injustice, oppression, and deprivation of dignity. Loretto considers it important not only to serve individual people and communities but also to work for systemic change. Loretto's status at the United Nations allows it to elevate the stories, experiences, and needs of people at the grassroots and use them to advocate for policies for peace and justice around the world. On the global stage, the voices of the people are essential for determining the true areas of need of the most vulnerable populations and for determining culturally appropriate and efficient implementation of policies. In an international system focused on efficiency and economic development, the Loretto Community NGO plays an important role in advocating for a human rights–based framework that respects the dignity and participation of all people.

In the long Loretto tradition of education, one of the most important objectives of the Loretto Community's work at the United Nations is to share information from the grassroots with UN delegates and NGO partners and the activities at the UN with the Loretto Community at large. In addition to traditional and social media and word-of-mouth, Loretto does this by inviting experts from the grassroots and members of its community to visit United Nations Headquarters and become active participants in meetings and dialogues. Every year, the Loretto Community invites dozens of students from its schools across the United States to come and participate in the annual Commission on the Status of Women. The students who attend return to their homes and schools with much greater awareness of the issues and challenges faced by girls and young women around the world, and they are inspired to work for the empowerment of women and girls both in their local communities and all over the world.

In the spring of 2012, Loretto at the UN coorganized and cosponsored two Women's Tribunals on Climate Justice, held in Central Appalachia and the Chicago metro area. The tribunals created a public space for women directly affected by poverty, climate change, and gender inequality to raise their voices and present testimony and to bring awareness and advocate for fundamental human rights. Women testified about their experiences living near mountaintop removal coal mining in Central Appalachia and living near coal-fired power plants and waste disposal sites on the outskirts of Chicago. They presented evidence of the destructive impact of coal mining and processing in their communities, including severe and widespread incidence of respiratory problems, birth defects, cancer, and other health conditions; reduced economic vitality; the alienation of communities; and local air, land and water pollution. After the testimony, distinguished jurists offered their policy recommendations to the witnesses and those in attendance. Loretto still actively engages with these issues at the UN, bringing these and similar stories to discussions about development and the protection of human rights. By highlighting the voices of the vulnerable, the Loretto Community is able to bring local, grassroots stories to the level of global advocacy, balancing and complementing the genuine concern for both the global and the local levels of policy reform.

Through advocacy on a wide variety of issues, the Loretto Community NGO promotes awareness and pursuit of human rights, protection of the sacredness of creation, and the establishment of systems and relationships in which all people are treated fairly and impartially.

STILL DOING WHAT NEEDS TO BE DONE
International Presentation Association

Mary Margaret Mooney, PBVM

Spirituality of the Sisters of the Presentation of the Blessed Virgin Mary is one of expanding awareness of the connection of all things in Christ. This process of evolution (unrolling of the mystery of God) lies at the heart of the spiritual story that their foundress Nano Nagle left as inheritance to all who follow the light of her lamp. Through the years this spirituality has led—sometimes in convoluted ways—to the sisters and associates doing what needed to be done in the arc of their skills and presence. In our times religious presence needs to be in the forum where global issues clash and converge. In our case this came to pass in the following way.

At a 1981 meeting in Rome, Superiors General of Congregations of Sisters of the Presentation of the Blessed Virgin Mary discussed ways to promote a worldwide concept of Presentation life and mission. Each of these congregations was a direct or indirect offshoot of Nano Nagle's original 1775 foundation in Cork, Ireland. In 1989 the International Presentation Association (IPA) was established.

As IPA found its identity and form, it became clear that Presentation charism and spirituality had universally found expression in a focus on justice as the centering force of mission and of ministry.

To facilitate communication in service of raising awareness and increasing effectiveness of action in areas of immediate need and systemic change, each unit—congregation, province, vice province, region—named a sister to serve as "justice contact." As individual sisters and units as a whole became more aware of the justice aspects of their work and more intentional about justice issues, the benefit of having a point of insertion at an international forum became apparent.

In 1995 a proposal was made for IPA to seek accredited NGO status at the United Nations in New York. In December of 1997, IPA was granted accreditation by the United Nations Department of Public Information. The process was then begun to seek special consultative status with the United Nations Economic and Social Council (ECOSOC). This status was achieved in 2000.

The International Presentation Association of the Sisters of the Presentation of the Blessed Virgin Mary (IPA) is a nonprofit entity incorporated in the State of New York. The mission of IPA is "to channel our resources so that we can speak and act in partnership with others for global justice." IPA is governed by a three-person board of directors. The IPA chief executive officer is the NGO director. The UN-accredited NGO is a ministry of the IPA.

The IPA NGO is not unique. The context of direct service which is the forte of apostolic congregations led them to see the need for systemic change, and one avenue for the latter is a presence at the United Nations. Thus, many religious congregations and collaborations thereof maintain a liaison office with the United Nations.

We are here not to chant a mantra of any currently "in" cause but to sing the hymn of continuing creation. For the PBVMs immersion in the founding principles of the United Nations is simply the here-and-now of doing what needs to be done to bring about the kingdom. Perhaps our efforts have helped make a little straighter the path to peace and freedom. Since its beginning, the issues on which IPA has focused have been those areas identified by Presentation sisters around the world as being most pertinent to our tradition and to the world we want to help create, namely, women and children, indigenous peoples, environment, and human rights.

The basic lessons IPA has learned are probably the same as those learned by all the other religious NGOs in New York and other UN sites. We have realized the need for the director to have sufficient time in orientation to learn the UN system. The UN is a foreign land with structures, language, and customs (protocols) all its own. To be missioned there requires preparation.

In the first few years we learned that the position of director of the IPA NGO needs to be full-time in order for that person to

- have time to study selected issues and speak with credibility,
- effectively participate in work of NGO committees and capitalize on networking opportunities with other NGOs,
- engage sisters whose ministries are enmeshed with the issues to which the NGO is attentive,
- facilitate involvement of unit leadership as appropriate, and
- heighten awareness of all sisters to their potential impact on matters of global concern.

We have learned to hold fast to principles, to rejoice in small achievements, to continue speaking and praying when confronted with injustices that seem immutable, to cling to the hope that the kingdom is here but not yet, and to be grounded in the realism expressed by the second Secretary-General of the United Nations: "The UN wasn't created to take mankind into paradise, but rather, to save humanity from hell."

With a universe of issues, problems, interests, and crisis, it is sometimes a challenge to maintain focus on selected issues. It is also a challenge to manage two-way communications with the people on the ground that bear the wounds the UN strives to bind up and who make real the lofty words of UN documents. It is a challenge not only to be *aware* that things move slowly at the UN but also to *accept* that results cannot be expected overnight.

Believing that the voices of those laboring to actualize in specific communities goals congruent with UN goals need to be heard in the realms of power, IPA has facilitated since 2007 participation in UN commissions, conferences, and other events for over a hundred people from fifteen countries. While the majority of these participants have been sisters, others—in particular girls and indigenous women—have been included. Participation has been not only at the New York site but also in Paris, France; Doha, Qatar; Melbourne, Australia; Bangkok, Thailand, Geneva, Switzerland; and Stockholm, Sweden.

Because of the work of these people and of the executive directors, IPA is a known entity to many member states—especially those in which Presentation sisters live and work. Letters from Zambian students in Presentation schools have been displayed in the UN visitors' lounge. Statements written by sisters have been translated into the official languages of the UN, read (hopefully) and archived by the UN. In addition to these written interventions, oral interventions have been made on immigration and other issues. CEDAW shadow reports have been written by Presentation people in Australia, Ireland, Canada, India, Thailand, and Peru. Nominees put forth by IPA for participation in a Social Development High Level Round Table were invited and full grants given for their participation. At least two Presentation projects have been identified as Best Practices and published by the NGO Committee on Social Development.

In a 2014 article published by the Leadership Conference of Women Religious, Fatima Rodrigo, then-executive director of IPA, made the following observations about aggregate accomplishments of the religious NGOs at the UN:

- Religious and other NGOs make a difference at the UN in influencing policies in support of people living in poverty and in favor of planet Earth.
- As the number and influence of NGOs have increased, there has been a shift in vision and language at the UN.

IPA is evolving as the UN evolves. Evolution is untidy. The dance of infinite possibility has a divine choreographer, but we are not always graceful in executing the steps. As we evolve both in our mission and in our understanding of creation, we plod along doing the best we can knowing that the metric by which we shall be measured is faithfulness not success, albeit a little of the latter would be appreciated.

EPILOGUE:

A Catholic NGO Reflection on Life, Leadership, and Community at United Nations

Joseph Cornelius Donnelly
Permanent Delegate to the United Nations
CARITAS Internationalis

Indeed, it is very good for us that they are here.

There are many challenging and competing realities present in and around the UN. Furthermore, there are as many controversies, political, social, religious, and logistical, as there are diplomatic fingerprints. The former UN Secretary-General Dag Hammarskjold often spoke about "markings." We have come to understand that it was his deep sense of the UN community and the international Family of Nations, this unique organization and its operational charter, that individually and collectively we "mark" personally but in countless different ways! Generally speaking, it is not a recorded documentation or PowerPoint presentation in a crammed conference room. It is a living witness of . . . "We, the peoples." In fact it can and should be a persistent bold witness underscoring the mission of larger freedom for all.

A CATHOLIC NGO REFLECTION ON LIFE AND COMMUNITY AT UNITED NATIONS

It is person-to-person diplomacy at its best . . . particularly when we engage the "other" as an exceptional, if ordinary, creature made in the image and likeness of God; every person, like every fingerprint bursting with valuable uniqueness. Through the seventy years of the UN as an intergovernmental body, people of faith have marked the development and perseverance of the institution in sometimes silent, sometimes dramatic ways. Members of our religious communities have stood out as pillars of faith, dignity, inclusiveness, and welcome to all.

The inspiration and tenacity of individual sisters, brothers, priests, and others like them, caring volunteers, have made important and sometimes remarkable differences. Their wisdom, compassion, and sense of the human family have been a steady source of energizing inspiration and community . . . in addition to often exceptional knowledge and experiences of the truly human condition.

Our ever-changing/always staying in the same UN neighborhood is "marked" more than ever by the gracious "hello, how are you," the exclamation of the latest journalistic commentary, and the proverbial "networking" which is a fundamental virtue, actionable Beatitude of the Catholic religious institutes as NGOs at the UN.

In the last century, the wise Trappist monk Thomas Merton wrote in his book *Bread in the Wilderness*, "Places like persons have an identity all their own, especially places like this one where people move from joy to sorrow and back again." He understood as our religious friends do that we exist together, we thrive together, and hopefully, we make our world a more sustainable, humane place to be for generations. The community of Catholic sisters, brothers, and priests mark the UN every day through its many uncertain seasons in New York and Geneva—as they do in remote places and major cities all around the world. It is easy to be grateful for such a blessing, for such abundance!

This *presence* educates us, teaches us, nourishes us, celebrates with us, and consoles us day by day.

ABOUT THE CONTRIBUTORS

Caroljean (Cj) Willie, SC, is a Sister of Charity of Cincinnati. She holds a Bachelor of Arts in Sociology, a master's degree in reading, and a PhD in multicultural education. She has worked cross-culturally throughout the United States, the Caribbean and Latin America, Africa, Asia, and Europe. She recently completed two terms of office as the NGO representative at the United Nations for the Sisters of Charity Federation and currently serves as the Program Director for Earth Connection, an environmental center in Cincinnati, Ohio.

Cecile Meijer, RSCJ, represents since 2003 the Society of the Sacred Heart at the United Nations. A national of the Netherlands, she studied and practiced law in the Netherlands and England, prior to moving to the USA. She holds an LL.M. degree specializing in International Protection of Human Rights, from the American University Washington College of Law in Washington, DC (USA).

Celine Paramundayil, MMS, is the UN representative of the Medical Mission Sisters. She holds a master's and MPhil in women's studies. Her passion and commitment to advocacy at the UN on behalf of the world's marginalized stem from her more than a decade long experience of working with the Dalits, the former untouchables in South India

Deirdre Mullan, RSM, PhD, is a Mercy sister from Ireland. Deirdre has worked at the United Nations since 2001 and currently is a consultant to UNICEF. She is working at identifying feeding programs run by religious congregations around the world with which UNICEF can collaborate.

Elizabeth Zwareva is a Maryknoll Sister native of Zimbabwe with mission experience in Bolivia and is now representing her congregation at the UN. Her passion and work interests are in areas of the integrity of creation—sustainable development, peace, security, and disarmament. Her calling is to work for peace, justice.

Emeka Xris Obiezu, OSA, is social justice animator and advocate. He has been part of the Augustinians International NGO's presence at the United Nations for more than ten years and currently serves as it main representative. He holds a PhD in political theology with specialty in Christian social responsibility, international development, and citizenship engagement.

Joan F. Burke, SNDdeN, served as the first representative of the Sisters of Notre Dame de Namur as an accredited NGO at the UN in New York (2002–2010), focusing primarily on social development and the eradication of poverty. Much of her life she has lived in different countries of Africa, and she is currently working in adult education in Kenya. By training, Joan is a social anthropologist (DPhil, Oxon.). Joan has served her congregation in a leadership role on both the general and intermediary levels.

John Paul Szura, OSA, is a priest of the Augustinian Order's Chicago Province. He was a seminary instructor in the United States, Peru, and the Philippines. John is a psychologist, a member of the American Psychological Association Division of Peace Psychology. He has been a member of the Augustinians UN–NGO team since its inception and is the director of the NGO's Canadian-Philippine's healthcare outreach.

Kevin Dance, CP, is an Australian member of the Passionist Congregation. He was the founding member of Passionists International as the body to represent the concerns of the Passionist family worldwide to the UN. He is presently living in Papua New Guinea and continues to have plenty of opportunity to follow his deep interest in human rights and the dignity of each person.

Marie Elena Dio, SC, Sister of Charity of Halifax, was the first UN representative for Federation of Sisters of Charity NGO and served fourteen years in this role. She was founding member of RUN and of NGO Committee on Financing for Development

(FfD). Marie was a former teacher/instructor on both high school and university levels with specialties in theology, interfaith understanding, and oriental history. Though presently "retired" she is still traveling and doing workshops on the UN and spirituality.

Mary Margaret Mooney, PBVM, professor emeritus of nursing at North Dakota State University, worked at the New York office of the International Presentation Association, 2014–2015. She currently works at a free health clinic in Mississippi.

Michele Morek, OSU, is an Ursuline Sister of Mount Saint Joseph, Kentucky (USA). She has a doctorate in biology from the University of Notre Dame, and most of her early professional ministries included teaching and administration at the college/university level. She served in community leadership for fourteen years, six of those as general superior. She has been the coalition coordinator of UNANIMA International since 2011.

Sally Dunne was appointed the United Nations NGO representative of the Loretto Community in 2008. She brought to the position a passion for equality and social and economic justice. With the leadership, knowledge, and skills acquired through experience in the business environment and in the educational arena, she developed a broad system approach to analyzing issues and solving problems. She is successfully using this approach in advocacy at the UN and in collaboration with other NGOs.